WELCOME

There's no ship quite like HMS *Belfast*.

No other vessel surviving in Britain today has witnessed historic events of the same magnitude. She took part in one of the greatest naval engagements of the Second World War; survived Arctic conditions to bring relief to Britain's ally, the Soviet Union; led the way on D-Day in 1944; and played a major role in Britain's support for the United Nations forces fighting in Korea from 1950 to 1952.

There's also no museum quite like HMS *Belfast*.

No other visitor experience is quite so physical and all-encompassing. You are walking the same decks, ducking through the same hatches and climbing up and down the same ladders that the men who served on board the ship would have done.

In this guidebook, you will read the story of *Belfast*'s quarter of a century of service and find out how all of her nine decks functioned together as one fighting machine. But more importantly, you will get to meet some of the men for whom the ship was home, and hear them tell their own experiences in their own words.

These are men who made enormous sacrifices to defend freedom, not just in Britain, but all over the world. Sometimes powerful, sometimes funny — always interesting — their stories deserve to be told. We hope you enjoy them.

THANK YOU
IWM tells the stories of those who have lived, fought and died in conflicts involving Britain and the Commonwealth since 1914. Every purchase ensures these stories are heard. Thank you, enjoy your visit and please come to see us again soon.

UPPER DECK 5

Flag Deck
Gun Direction Platform

5

UPPER DECK 4

Compass Platform
Operations Room

4

UPPER DECK 3

40 / 60 Gun Deck
Admiral's Bridge
Admiral's and Captain's Sea Cabins
Bridge Wireless Office (BWO)
Electronic Warfare Office (EWO)

3

UPPER DECK 2

B-Turret
Officers' Sea Cabins

2

UPPER DECK 1

4-inch HA / LA Mountings
A-Turret
Boat Deck
Fo'c'sle

Toilets 🚹 🚺
The Café 🍴

1

2

MAIN DECK 0

Arctic Messdecks
Gun Turret Experience (Y-Turret)
Quarterdeck

Exhibitions

Life at Sea
War and Peace

Accessible Lift ♿
Virtual Tour
Toilets 🚹 🚺 ♿ 🚼
Information ℹ
Audioguides 🎧

Quayside

Shop 🛍
Tickets 🎫
Tom's Kitchen Deli 🍴
Tom's Kitchen Bar 🍸

0

LOWER DECK -1

Boiler Room
Engine Room

-1

LOWER DECK -2

Boiler Room
Engine Room
Forward Steering Position
Shell Rooms

-2

LOWER DECK -3

Boiler Room
Engine Room

-3

CONTENTS

When you step off the gangway on to HMS *Belfast*, you are following a path trodden by thousands of officers and men, who lived, fought and even died on board the ship. This is the story of their exploits.

Your tour of the ship begins on this level. Most of the main exhibition areas are here and it's where the ship's crew lived much of their everyday lives.

Beneath the Main Deck sit three lower levels. Head down here and you will discover the inner workings of the ship, including her huge engine and boiler rooms and her stores of ammunition and explosives.

Five more levels sit above the Main Deck, starting with the open spaces of the 'Upper Deck' and ending in the heights of the 'Flag Deck' at the top of the ship. These decks were home to the 'brains' of HMS *Belfast*.

IN THEIR OWN WORDS

At the end of each of the four sections of the guidebook, you'll find the words, stories and memories of veterans who served on board HMS *Belfast* — some taken from a diary entry or a letter home, others from interviews recorded with members of IWM staff. They paint a vivid picture of what it was like to witness history as it unfolded, or to live and work in a particular section of the ship.

HMS *Belfast* is a warship designed for active service at sea. Please take great care as you tour the ship, especially on the ladders. Look out for overhead and floor-level hazards. Areas may be closed for conservation.

ESSENTIAL BELFAST

Exploring HMS *Belfast* is an experience in itself, climbing up and down ladders, feeling the ship moving beneath your feet and encountering all sorts of sights, sounds and smells along the way. But we think there are some particular *Belfast* experiences that shouldn't be missed.

HEAD INTO BATTLE

Our thrilling **Gun Turret Experience: A Sailor's Story, 1943** transports you back to the day HMS *Belfast* helped to sink the German battle cruiser *Scharnhorst*. Experience what it was like to be in the heart of the action as lights, imagery, smoke effects, vibrations, sounds and smells re-create the intense atmosphere of battle inside a cramped gun turret.

IWM BELF665

GO TO THE RESCUE

Head up to the **Operations Room** and help recover a downed plane from the sea off the coast of North Borneo — an operation based on a real-life exercise carried out by the ship in 1961. Take control not only of *Belfast* but of an entire fleet of ships, using touch screen plotting tables to relay your commands. Can you stay focussed while, all around you, radar screens and equipment lights flare into life, re-creating the sights and sounds of the ship's nerve centre at work?

IWM BELF616

BECOME CAPTAIN

Make your way to the **Compass Platform** and take a seat on the captain's chair. You'll soon find that it's not a position built for comfort, but as you look at the array of instruments all around, you'll get an idea of what it must have been like to command HMS *Belfast* and to safeguard the lives of her thousand-strong crew.

IWM BELF552

FEEL THE POWER

Say goodbye to the comfort of daylight and descend into the **Boiler and Engine Rooms** deep in the heart of the ship. Marvel at the complexity and scale of the machinery that powered *Belfast* into battle, and imagine working down here in the heat of a tropical summer, trying to ignore the relentless noise all around you, and knowing that you are under the waterline if anything goes wrong.

IWM BELF750

FIND A PLACE TO SLEEP

Visit the **Arctic Messdeck** to get a sense of what it was like to live on board *Belfast* during the Second World War. See the tightly-packed hammocks, slung just 52cm apart, and listen to the words of a genuine letter home written by a sailor relaxing between watches.

IWM BELF335

THE STORY OF HMS BELFAST

HMS *Belfast* was no sooner commissioned into the Royal Navy than she was at war. In a matter of weeks, her newly appointed crew of 761 men and officers went from performing sea trials to hunting down enemy raiders attempting to break out of the North Sea into the Atlantic.

They were also tasked with imposing a maritime blockade on Germany, stopping and searching merchant vessels to prevent would-be soldiers or contraband supplies reaching the enemy. And they soon distinguished themselves, boarding and capturing the biggest merchant ship taken in the war to that date — the German *Cap Norte* — which was travelling in the guise of a neutral Swedish vessel named SS *Ancona*.

In the first month of the war alone, HMS *Belfast* and the rest of the 18th Cruiser Squadron stopped, searched and sent into port for inspection no fewer than 48 vessels. The German war machine would need to look elsewhere for its supplies.

DID YOU KNOW?

King George VI had a small head. While having lunch on HMS *Belfast* in 1943, the story goes that he hung his Admiral's cap outside the wardroom, but few of the men who queued up to try it on could get it to fit.

7

Launching day (left)
HMS *Belfast* runs down the slipway at the Harland & Wolff shipyard to the cheers of workers and their families.
IWM HU43755

Champagne moment (left)
The ribbon from the bottle of champagne used to launch *Belfast* on St Patrick's Day, 17 March 1938.
IWM BELF384

THE ROLE OF A CRUISER

HMS *Belfast* was a cruiser, smaller than a battleship but larger than a destroyer. Like all cruisers, she was designed to patrol the seas, guarding friendly ships, providing support for larger warships, preying on enemy cargo vessels and engaging enemy cruisers where necessary.

Traditionally, a cruiser's strength was her combination of speed and cruising radius, allowing her to cover large areas of ocean and react quickly to enemy threats. But by the mid-1930s, when *Belfast* was being built, a cruiser also had to be heavily armoured to withstand enemy attack and carry enough firepower to pack a worthwhile punch. HMS *Belfast*, then, became one of the first and most powerful of a new class of 'large light cruisers' – a class that would serve Britain long after the Second World War.

Commissioned into the Navy (left)
On joining the fleet, HMS *Belfast* had to swap the red ensign of the merchant service for the white of the Royal Navy. Unfortunately, the red ensign became stuck and had to be unjammed by hand.   IWM HU4645

OCTOBER 1939: UNDER THREAT

8

The first few months of the Second World War were dubbed the 'Phoney War' by a press surprised by the lack of action on land. But there was nothing phoney about the war at sea. Just hours after hostilities began, a British liner had been torpedoed and sunk by a German U-boat in the Atlantic, and HMS *Belfast* faced the same threat every time she put to sea.

Even her anchorage at Scapa Flow, the Royal Navy's main base in the Orkney Islands, north of Scotland, proved to be no safe haven. In the early hours of 14 October 1939, the German submarine *U-47* mounted a daring raid into the heart of the harbour and sank the battleship *Royal Oak* with the loss of 833 lives. The Home Fleet was immediately dispersed, with *Belfast* being sent to Rosyth in the Firth of Forth. But danger was never far away and HMS *Belfast* herself would soon become the target.

NOVEMBER 1939: KNOCK-OUT BLOW

A gentle breeze and blue skies greeted *Belfast* as she headed out of the Firth of Forth for gunnery exercises on the morning of 21 November 1939. Then, at 10:52, there was a violent explosion.

Steel, machinery, rivets, bone and sinew were caught in a convulsion that broke the ship's back, put her engines out of action and injured 21 men, one fatally.

HMS *Belfast* had fallen victim to one of Hitler's secret new weapons – the magnetic mine, a submerged explosive device activated by the steel hull of any passing ship. She would be out of the war for almost three years.

HMS BELFAST TIMELINE
The construction of HMS *Belfast* was completed just in time for the outbreak of the Second World War. She would go on to serve with distinction for over a quarter of a century, before taking up the position that she occupies today on the banks of the River Thames.

17 MARCH 1938
HMS *Belfast* is launched on St Patrick's Day. The ceremony is carried out in Belfast by the wife of Prime Minister Neville Chamberlain.

5 AUGUST 1939
After 18 months of fitting out and sea trials, HMS *Belfast* is commissioned for service in the Royal Navy

DECEMBER 1942: BACK IN ACTION

By the time HMS *Belfast* rejoined the fleet in December 1942, the war in Europe had changed. Britain was under siege, her army driven from the continent, her cities devastated by bombing raids. France had long since fallen, and Hitler's troops were deep into Russian territory.

HMS *Belfast* had changed too. She hadn't just been repaired, she had been redesigned and rebuilt to become the largest and arguably the most powerful cruiser in the Royal Navy. And she would need to be, because she was about to embark on the most active period of her life.

Damage to the hull (above)
A photograph taken in dry dock in 1940 shows the shockwave damage caused when a magnetic mine detonated beneath *Belfast* in late 1939
IWM MH23670

DID YOU KNOW?

Tragically, after *Belfast* was mined, some of her Royal Marines and Boy Seamen were transferred to HMS *Hood*, which was sunk in May 1941 with the loss of all but three of her 1,418-strong crew.

3 SEPTEMBER 1939
Britain and France declare war on Germany (right) following the German invasion of Poland
IWM HU36171

OCTOBER 1939
During her first weeks on patrol, **HMS *Belfast*** captures a disguised German vessel called the *Cap Norte*

21 NOVEMBER 1939
HMS *Belfast* is put out of action when a magnetic mine — one of Adolf Hitler's new secret weapons — explodes beneath her hull

FEBRUARY 1943: CONVOY ESCORT

By this point, one of the vital aims of the war at sea was to keep supply lines open to the Soviet Union, in the hope that she would be able to take the fight to Hitler on Germany's eastern front. In 1942 alone, convoys of merchant ships, escorted mainly by ships of the Royal Navy's Home Fleet, had delivered 6,714 tanks, 15,600 aircraft, 85,000 vehicles and 70 million rounds of small arms ammunition to their Soviet allies.

But it was no easy task. Conditions in the Arctic were appalling: so cold that metal and skin would freeze tight against each other in an instant; so dark in the winter that dawn and dusk were only an hour or two apart; seas so mountainous that a gun turret roof could be ripped off by the force of a single wave.

And for every second of every hour of every day, the men of the merchant ships and their naval protectors knew that they were only a torpedo or shell away from a freezing death. Such was the life awaiting HMS *Belfast* in February 1943, when she began work as an escort ship.

DID YOU KNOW?

HMS *Belfast* has a twin. She was HMS *Edinburgh*, built to the same design as *Belfast* but torpedoed and sunk in May 1942 while escorting a convoy in the Arctic Ocean.

First run (above)
HMS *Belfast* leaves Iceland in February 1943 for her first round-trip to the Soviet Union.
IWM A15530

Hurricane force (above)
HMS *Belfast* encounters heavy seas on her way to the Soviet Union in 1943. Conditions were so treacherous that six of the ships in the convoy had to turn back, including *Belfast*'s sister ship HMS *Sheffield*.
IWM HU9144

JUNE 1940
The British Expeditionary Force is evacuated from France at Dunkirk (right). Britain is under siege.
IWM H1623

JUNE 1941
Hitler launches Operation Barbarossa — the invasion of the Soviet Union

10 DECEMBER 1942
After three long years of work at Devonport Dockyard, the repairs on **HMS *Belfast*** are finally complete

Battle against the ice

Sailors and Royal Marines take a break from their
ice clearing duties on the decks of HMS *Belfast*,
November 1943. Apart from putting guns and fire
control systems out of action, a build-up of ice
could make the ship top-heavy and unstable.

IWM HU8799

DECEMBER 1943: THE BATTLE OF NORTH CAPE

All Russian convoys were suspended in the summer of 1943, as the growing hours of daylight made the threat of air attack too great. When they were resumed in November, three eastbound and two westbound convoys were able to get through with no losses, thanks in part to the breaking of Germany's 'Enigma' code. Hitler's naval chief, Admiral Doenitz, put pressure on the Führer to approve the unleashing of one of the navy's big beasts – the battle cruiser *Scharnhorst* – to attack the next two convoys. The scene was set for one of *Belfast*'s finest hours: the Battle of North Cape.

Scharnhorst put to sea on Christmas Day, her mess decks still adorned with decorations. By 03:39 the next morning, the Admiralty had got wind of the German orders and

were able to arrange the British ships accordingly. One group, called Force 1, including the cruisers *Belfast*, *Norfolk* and *Sheffield*, would stay with the convoys, ready to engage *Scharnhorst* as soon as they made contact. A second group, Force 2, led by the battleship *Duke of York*, would approach from the south, ready to cut off *Scharnhorst*'s likely escape route.

At 08:40, after a tense five-hour wait, HMS *Belfast* detected *Scharnhorst* on her radar. Forty minutes later sixteen-year-old John Crossman, manning one of *Belfast*'s 4-inch guns, was ordered to fire starshell to light the German ship up. *Norfolk* then unleashed a series of salvoes, hitting *Scharnhorst* and, crucially, putting her radar out of action. The German giant slipped back into the darkness.

21 FEBRUARY 1943
HMS *Belfast* begins work as an escort ship for the convoys crossing the Arctic Ocean to and from the Soviet Union

26 DECEMBER 1943
Belfast plays a key role in the Battle of North Cape, during which the mighty *Scharnhorst* is sunk

MARCH 1944
HMS *Belfast* takes part in Operation Tungsten – the Allied attempt to sink the German battleship *Tirpitz*

At 12:21, *Sheffield* had *Scharnhorst* in her sights again. The two sides traded blows through the driving snow and rain, *Belfast* firing twelve broadsides in three minutes alone, and *Norfolk* being hit twice with seven fatalities. Then from the bridge of HMS *Belfast*, Vice-Admiral Burnett ordered his cruisers to cease fire: *Scharnhorst* was on the retreat and, blinded by the damage to her radar, she was heading directly towards the awaiting *Duke of York*. The trap was set.

It was vital that the ships of Force 1 stay in radar contact with *Scharnhorst*. That way they could report her evasive manoeuvres to *Duke of York*. But by 16:03 *Norfolk* had to reduce speed to put out a fire and seven minutes later *Sheffield* too had to drop back with engine trouble. HMS *Belfast* was alone and extremely vulnerable; if *Scharnhorst* turned back, she had more than enough firepower to sink the British cruiser and make good her escape.

But by 16:17 it was too late. The *Duke of York* had picked her up and by 18:00 the British battleship had landed mighty blows with her first and third salvoes. The game was up, but *Scharnhorst* would go down fighting as the British destroyers – and then cruisers – moved in for the kill. No one saw the moment when she sank beneath the waves. She was spotted at 19:38 by *Jamaica* but when *Belfast* ran in for another attack she came across only wreckage, smoke and a few survivors. The battle was over.

DID YOU KNOW?
There was an antelope on board *Belfast* during the Battle of North Cape. It was a gift to the ship from the Russians, but the noise of the guns drove it mad and it had to be put down.

Running the gauntlet (left)
Battle cruisers *Scharnhorst* and *Gneisenau* make a run for home from the French port of Brest – an incident later known as the 'Channel Dash', 12 February 1942. IWM MH4981

Grand old *Duke of York* (below)
HMS *Duke of York* fires her 14-inch guns as waves crash over her decks. The British battleship was the key player in the sinking of *Scharnhorst*. IWM A7550

13

MARCH 1944: FINISHING THE JOB

After losing *Scharnhorst*, the Germans had only one more heavy battleship, *Tirpitz*, to pit against the British fleet. And even she was a wounded animal, badly damaged by a midget submarine attack in September 1943. But she remained a threat and the Admiralty were keen to finish her off.

This time, the plan was to hit her from above with bombers and fighters launched from aircraft carriers off the Norwegian coast. HMS *Belfast* was among a large fleet of cruisers and destroyers tasked with defending the vital carriers from surface attack.

The raid succeeded in putting *Tirpitz* out of action for several more months before she was finally sunk by a force of heavy bombers in November 1944. The war at sea was being won. Now it was time to renew hostilities on the continental mainland.

JUNE 1944: D-DAY

At 05:27 on 6 June 1944, the German garrison in the Normandy town of Ver-sur-Mer woke to find themselves trapped in a deadly firestorm. They, and their four 10cm howitzer guns, were target number one for a ferocious *Belfast* broadside.

For two hours, they cowered beneath salvo after salvo of 6-inch shells, leaving them powerless to defend their beach from the massive amphibious assault that followed. When 7th Battalion, Green Howards, overran their position later that morning, the shell-shocked Germans were all too ready to surrender.

DID YOU KNOW?
HMS *Belfast* was supposed to fire the first shots of D-Day, but another trigger-happy ship stole her thunder by about a minute.

CHURCHILL'S PLANS THWARTED

A few days before the Normandy landings, Prime Minister Winston Churchill informed the Admiralty that he intended to witness the operation first-hand from the decks of HMS *Belfast*. The idea of letting the country's wartime leader put himself in such danger was preposterous but Churchill was more than ready to pull rank to get his way. In the end, the problem was solved when King George VI called Churchill's bluff, saying that if his Prime Minister was going, then he ought to go too, as head of the three Services. This was a risk that even Churchill was not prepared to take, so the plan was quietly shelved.

Heading to the front (left)
Prime Minister Winston Churchill was eventually taken to the Normandy coast on board HMS *Kelvin* on 12 June 1944, at a time when conditions were still extremely dangerous. IWM EA26227

6 JUNE 1944	JULY 1944	8 MAY 1945	
HMS *Belfast* helps to lead the bombardment that precedes Operation Overlord – the Allied invasion of France	As the Allied troops push inland from the Normandy coast, *Belfast* begins a refit for duty in the Far East	Millions celebrate 'Victory in Europe' Day (right). The following month *Belfast* sets out on her voyage to the Far East. IWM EA65799	

This was Operation Overlord — the long-awaited Allied invasion of Nazi-occupied France. Overnight HMS *Belfast* had cruised along the English Channel to take up position six miles off the French coast. It was her role to lead the naval force assigned to bombard two of the five beaches chosen for the landings.

As she — and all the other bombardment vessels — opened fire, a further 4,600 ships, boats and smaller craft waited further out, ready to deliver troops and supplies to shore. At 07:30 the first wave of landing craft surged past *Belfast* to cheers of support from her crew. By nightfall Allied troops had established a firm foothold along a 50-mile stretch of the shoreline.

For the next six days, HMS *Belfast* fired close to 2,000 rounds at fortified positions, enemy batteries and troop concentrations. All the while, the bombardment force was itself a target for U-boats, human torpedoes, motor torpedo boats, mines, shore-based batteries and dive-bomber attacks. *Belfast* veterans report a number of close shaves, with nearby ships being hit and shrapnel searing its way into the deck.

Belfast's Sick Bay remained active from day one. The first casualties, soldiers from the shore, arrived at 13:00, and the ship's surgeons worked around the clock — often in vain — to save them. All too often bodies were seen floating back from the shore past the bows of the watchful cruiser.

For five weeks, HMS *Belfast* supported Allied troops as they fought their way inland. It was 8 July when she fired her guns in anger for the last time in European waters. Her final bombardment helped bring about the fall of Caen, after which the front line moved beyond the range of her guns. It was time for a change of role.

Lighting up the night
HMS *Belfast* provided weeks of bombardment support for Allied forces in Normandy after D-Day. Here her starboard 4-inch guns open fire against German shore positions on the night of 27 June 1944.
IWM A24325

6 AUGUST 1945
The atomic bomb is dropped on Hiroshima. A second falls on Nagasaki three days later (right). Japan is ready to surrender. The war is over.
IWM MH2629

1946-1948
HMS *Belfast* helps to keep the fragile peace in the Far East

APRIL-JULY 1949
HMS *Belfast* oversees attempts to free HMS *Amethyst*, trapped by Chinese forces on the Yangtze River

1945-1949:
HEADING EAST

As the Allied armies bore down on Berlin, *Belfast* underwent a refit to prepare her for a new theatre of war. By April 1945 she was undergoing sea trials and by June she was heading out of home waters to start the long journey east to the Pacific.

Just days before she reached Australia, news filtered through of the atomic bomb strikes on Hiroshima and Nagasaki, and Japan's surrender. Needless to say, the ship enjoyed a raucous reception in Sydney.

But what lived longer in the memories of *Belfast*'s crewmen were the looks on the faces of the British families they helped to liberate from the civilian internment camps in Shanghai. When it was discovered that some of the children had never tasted chocolate before, there wasn't a man's locker on board that remained unscoured.

APRIL 1949:
THE YANGTZE INCIDENT

The hard-won peace in the Far East was an uneasy one. China in particular was in turmoil, with Mao Zedong leading his Communist forces towards the eventual overthrow of Chiang Kai-shek's Nationalist government in October 1949. The world watched anxiously in fear that the conflict would spread more widely.

Tensions peaked in April of that year as a British warship *Amethyst* was attacked and disabled by Mao Zedong's forces as she steamed down the Yangtze River. The stricken vessel was to spend six weeks trapped some 100 miles from help, and HMS *Belfast*, from her anchorage in Hong Kong, was to play a crucial role in her escape.

It was from *Belfast*'s radio room that coded messages were relayed to and from *Amethyst*, and it was at 18:30 on 30 July that a garbled message eventually came through to say that the trapped ship was going to make a run for it at 22:00. A dinner party for local dignitaries

HMS BELFAST BECOMES A PARTY SHIP

In October 1945 the officers and men of HMS *Belfast* decided to hold a party on board to entertain British children newly liberated from Japanese internment camps. By the time the guests were piped aboard, the ship's decks had been ingeniously transformed into a playground, with see-saws, roundabouts and a swing. And for the real thrill-seekers, the crew had rigged up a chairlift from the Flag Deck down to the Boat Deck. It was a great success. One eleven-year-old boy, Ian Pearson, enjoyed the party so much he decided there and then that he would one day join the Navy – and he did.

Swinging success (left)
Members of HMS *Belfast*'s crew lift some young party guests out of an improvised swing, made from a storage crate suspended from the ship's crane.
IWM A30854

1 OCTOBER 1949
The Chinese Civil War ends when Communist Mao Zedong declares a new People's Republic of China

25 JUNE 1950
Communist North Korean forces invade independent South Korea, beginning the Korean War. UN-mandated forces are sent to defend South Korea.

JUNE-OCTOBER 1950
The *Belfast* patrols the waters of the Yellow Sea, providing bombardment support for UN troops on land

1951-1952
As the war drags on, **HMS Belfast** returns to action along the west coast of Korea, and is hit on 29 July 1952 (right)
IWM HU36642

had been arranged on board HMS *Belfast* for that night, and Admiral Brind decided that it should go ahead to allay any suspicions that something was afoot. At 21:30 he raised a toast to 'HMS *Amethyst* and all who sail in her' and invited his guests to enjoy coffee and liqueurs on the Quarterdeck.

In the meantime signal pads and maps replaced dinner plates and wine glasses on the Admiral's table and a tense night of waiting ensued. At 22:35 came the message: 'I am under fire and have been hit', but by 01:00 *Amethyst* had managed to reach the halfway mark and by dawn she was home and dry — much to the relief of the Admiral hunched over his maps in the stern of *Belfast*.

Shore bombardment (right)
Two of HMS *Belfast*'s 6-inch gun turrets fire a salvo at shore targets in North Korea in November 1951. *Belfast* was one of scores of British ships supporting UN forces.
IWM A32031

1950-1952: WAR IN KOREA

China wasn't the only country in the Far East caught in crisis at this time. Korea was split down the middle with a hard-line communist regime in the north and a more moderate government in the south, supported by the United Nations. Perhaps emboldened by the success of the Communists in China, North Korea decided to invade the South on 25 June 1950.

The war sparked by this unwarranted act of aggression would see HMS *Belfast* fire more shells than she did in the whole of the Second World War. She even had to have her 6-inch guns replaced part-way through the conflict after wearing them out providing constant support for the troops on land. So accurate was her gunnery — and so quick — that the Americans christened her 'that straight-shooting ship' and could hardly believe that her guns were partially hand-worked.

In all, *Belfast* put in 404 days of active service during the war, operating close in to the enemy-occupied shoreline in order to extend her range inland. She was hit only once in that time, on 29 July 1952, when a 76mm shell from a battery on the island of Wolsa-ri punched through her side, killing a Chinese rating and wounding four others. The small patched-up section of the hull can still be seen on *Belfast*'s starboard side.

By this stage the war had slipped into a protracted stalemate that would eventually end with an armistice agreement in July 1953. HMS *Belfast*'s days of wartime service ended somewhat sooner: on 27 September 1952 she was on her way home to Britain.

4 NOVEMBER 1952
HMS *Belfast* arrives back in Britain and faces the possibility of being consigned to the scrap heap

27 JULY 1953
After months of stalemate, an Armistice Agreement is signed to end the fighting in Korea

MARCH 1955
The decision is taken to modernise **HMS *Belfast*** and keep her in the fleet

1952-1959:
AN UNCERTAIN FUTURE

When HMS *Belfast* arrived home, she was placed into reserve, which left her only a short step away from the scrapyard. She remained in this limbo state for almost three years, while debate rumbled on over the role that Britain and her Navy should play in world affairs.

For Britain, there was the issue of how to manage the gradual transfer of independence to her colonies. And for her Navy, there was the challenge of the new atomic age — what good were the guns of a warship against an ever-proliferating arsenal of nuclear missiles?

Eventually it was decided that *Belfast* still had a role to play — as support for the Navy's aircraft carriers, and as an ambassador for Britain in foreign waters.

1959-1962:
FINAL YEARS AT SEA

Between 1956 and 1959 HMS *Belfast* was rebuilt for her new future — most notably gaining a fully enclosed bridge and a modern air conditioning system, so that the entire ship could be sealed against atomic, biological or chemical attack.

Thankfully these defences would never be required. Apart from some peacetime exercises, *Belfast*'s two final foreign commissions involved only a whistlestop tour of the world's great ports — ending with a remarkable circumnavigation of the globe, taking in Guam, Hawaii, San Francisco, Seattle, British Columbia, the Panama Canal and Trinidad.

It was on 19 June 1962 that she reached Portsmouth for the final time to be greeted, as ever, by a waiting crowd of families and friends. A bugle sounded and, turning forward and aft, the files of crewmen on the upper deck were dismissed. After almost half a million miles of steaming, HMS *Belfast* was home.

1962-1971:
TOWARDS A NEW ROLE

On 14 April 1967, a team from the Imperial War Museum visited Portsmouth to look into acquiring one of HMS *Gambia*'s 6-inch gun turrets. They were served lunch on board HMS *Belfast*, which by that time had become a Harbour Accommodation Ship. By the end of the meal, the idea of preserving an entire ship had been born — and HMS *Belfast* was the perfect candidate.

The plan almost foundered in February 1971 when the government rejected the museum's proposal, but a charitable trust, led by one of *Belfast*'s former captains, stepped in to save the day. Eight months later, on 21 October 1971, Trafalgar Day, HMS *Belfast* was opened to the public. In 1978 the Imperial War Museum was allowed to take over its operation.

Care and attention (above)
A rare view of HMS *Belfast*'s mighty propellers, seen when the ship went into dry dock in 1982 for conservation work.
IWM 19824040

1959-1962	**19 JUNE 1962**	**JULY 1971**	**21 OCTOBER 1971**
After an extensive refit, **HMS Belfast** embarks on two commissions in the Far East	After 25 years of service, **HMS Belfast** returns home for the final time. A year later she is placed into reserve.	On the verge of disposal, **Belfast** is handed over to the Belfast Trust with the aim of preserving her for the nation	On Trafalgar Day, at her new berth on the banks of the Thames, **HMS Belfast** opens to members of the public for the first time

Coming home
Tower Bridge opens to allow HMS
Belfast to pass through into the Pool
of London on 15 October 1971.
IWM MH15061

In their own words

Throughout *Belfast*'s service thousands of her officers and men bore witness to history as it was being made. Here, a few of them tell their version of events — as recorded in letters, diaries or later interviews.

FIRST CONTACT

Veteran George Woodley, was at the helm of HMS *Belfast* when she claimed her first notable capture in the Second World War — stopping and boarding a German ship attempting to reach its homeland under the guise of a Swedish flag.

I'll never forget. *Belfast* was on northern patrol between Iceland and the Shetlands when a large ship was sighted (we had no radar in those days). The speed was increased to full power. It was exhilarating, steering this new ship at over 32 knots — I could feel the power of her engines!

We carefully approached a 13,000 ton cargo liner flying the Swedish flag. Two seaboats were launched, crewed by seamen and stokers and manned by armed Marines. The boarding parties were sent over to board the vessel.

The ship rolled gently and as the sun shone on her side, the name on the bows was seen to be freshly painted. She was not Swedish but a German liner named '*Cap Norte*', with a valuable cargo. The boarding crew took the prize to Scapa Flow under escort.

BELFAST IS MINED

John Harrison was at his post in 'A' Gun Turret when a magnetic mine detonated beneath the bows of HMS *Belfast*. He recalls the explosion and the immediate aftermath when water began to pour into the confined space of his action station.

A terrific thud and I felt my spine going into my skull and everything went dark . . . Dead silence. Followed by a shaking up and down as though you were shaking a doll and then it went very quiet . . .

I said we'd better try to get out of here and the only way is up through this little hatch between the right-hand and centre gun. Trying to force that up, water came in. Now, in virtual pitch black you think, right, we're sunk.

Anyway we managed to get this thing open and it was the drenching gear that had been distorted by the force of the explosion and was facing straight down this hatch — much to our relief.

Holding fire (right)
Members of a gun crew pose with their shells in the days after the Battle of North Cape, December 1943.
IWM A13973

> '*Scharnhorst* pumped out everything she'd got to stave off the attack. She was like a cornered rat.'

HUNTING SCHARNHORST

About a year after HMS *Belfast* rejoined the war as an Arctic convoy escort ship, she played a crucial role in sinking the German battle cruiser *Scharnhorst*. Here gunnery officer Lieutenant W P Brooke Smith **recalls the closing hours of the action.**

For two hours we continued the chase alone – well within her gun-range. It was unreal – seeing the enemy only when illuminated by starshell and seeing her gunflashes. We got two or three near misses. That's a funny feeling when you see the fountains of water rising, and the guns fire again with a corrected salvo!

When *Scharnhorst* ran into the *Duke of York*, *Duke*'s orange-red gunflashes and *Scharnhorst*'s greeny-yellow ones occupied the sky. In the darkness, as it was possible she might still escape, the 'boats' were sent in. That destroyer attack is the bravest and most thrilling thing I've ever seen. *Scharnhorst* pumped out everything she'd got to stave off the attack. She was like a cornered rat. A big fire broke out – it must have been living hell.

D-DAY DANGER

Peter Rudd **was an able seaman on board HMS *Belfast* at the time of the Normandy landings. Here he recalls the fate of another Royal Navy ship – a fate which *Belfast* herself could so easily have shared.**

We saw a destroyer approaching. When she was abreast of us and about a hundred yards away, there was a massive explosion amidships and she broke in two. We immediately had scrambling nets over the side and started to rescue survivors.

NORMANDY LANDINGS

Belfast crewman **A Jones** grabbed a few moments on the day after D-Day to write a letter to his family in Stoke-on-Trent describing the extraordinary events that he had witnessed.

When we came along the English Channel we passed thousands of landing craft, of all shapes and sizes, and all the boys were cheering. And as we approached the coast of France we could hear thousands of bombers overhead and then all along the coast there were loud explosions and great fires.

We went in first with the invasion barges behind us, and then came the great moment when we opened fire. When we had finished shelling the beach, all the invasion craft surged forward and landed and they seem to be making splendid progress.

We haven't seen any U-boats or E boats yet, but we had a few air attacks, which we soon drove away, all yesterday. We shelled the German shore batteries and put nearly all of them out of action. We are just going to start another bombardment, so I shall have to close now.

ON THE BEACHES

'I landed in France on the seat of my pants!'

In the weeks following D-Day, the crew of HMS *Belfast* didn't carry out all of their duties at sea. As veteran **R W Brown** explains, they were also sent ashore in DUKW amphibious vehicles ('ducks') to do their bit – a risky business in more ways than one . . .

After several weeks, the beach was covered in debris and we were taken to an area needing a clean up. The 'duck' I was in pulled up on the sand to disconnect the propeller and engage the gears. I stood up on the back to get a view when the 'duck' jerked forward and I landed in France on the seat of my pants!

And more seriously . . . The Germans had a mobile gun at the northern end of the beachhead, which harassed the activity on the beach and on the anchored ships. One of its shells landed in shallow water about 50 yards from us. As it exploded, we prostrated ourselves and the shrapnel rattled off the side of the beached landing craft behind us.

Opening the front (far right)
British commandos wade ashore as part of the opening wave of D-Day landings.
IWM B5103

Grandstand view (right)
Rear-Admiral Dalrymple-Hamilton watches events unfold in the early hours of 6 June 1944 from the bridge of HMS *Belfast*. Smoking a pipe in the background is Frederick Parham, captain of *Belfast*.
IWM HU65372

'*When we had finished shelling the beach, all the invasion craft surged forward and landed.*'

TAKING RISKS IN HIROSHIMA

A few months after HMS *Belfast* arrived in the Far East, Charles Quinlan **remembers visiting Hiroshima, scene of the atomic bomb blast that brought the Second World War to an abrupt end. Even close to a year later, it was still a place of danger — both visible and invisible.**

It was impossible to believe that one bomb could have caused so much damage. While passing the remains of a building, people were attempting to free someone who had been trapped by a falling wall. We went to help.

When the atomic bomb was dropped, most of the glass melted into rivulets. The colours created by the molten glass were really quite lovely. We collected some . . . and eventually took it back to the UK. Of course, what we didn't know then was the devastating effect of radiation, otherwise we wouldn't have touched it. I often wonder if the *Belfast* glowed at night with all that radioactive material on board!

`'I often wonder if the Belfast glowed at night with all that radioactive material on board!'`

Christmas cheer (right) Crewmen of HMS *Belfast* celebrate Christmas Day 1951 off the coast of Korea. It proved a busy 'holiday' period with the ship subjecting some troublesome North Korean batteries to regular bombardment.

IWM HU36593

THE BATTLE OF CHANGNI-DO

Towards the end of her second period of service in the Korean War, HMS *Belfast* – together with HMS *Amethyst* – helped to recapture the island of Changni-do. The story is told in the Commission Book put together to mark the end of the crew's time on the ship.

Suddenly . . . came the news that the island had been invaded by the enemy during the night. We immediately closed and Lieutenant Morris and his merry men pushed off on a reconnaissance.

> '*Taking advantage of our larger guns, we got out of their probable range, and let them have it.*'

DID YOU KNOW?

The sailors of HMS *Belfast* used to cool off in the shark-infested waters of the Far East by swimming inside a big net attached to the ship.

As they nosed inshore they were met with machine-gun fire and Marine Coffin was wounded. They returned fire themselves with interest; but this was more than impertinence and we began to bombard. By this time the USS *Bataan*'s strike aircraft were coming in under *Belfast*'s control, and between us all we gave the enemy a hot time of it.

Towards evening a battery on the mainland began firing on *Amethyst*. While we were observing this with more than a little interest, another battery began firing at us! Indignantly, taking advantage of our larger guns, we got out of their probable range, and let them have it.

The conditions were almost ideal. There was an obliging green slope up to where the flashes were coming from, and our first shot made a nice brown mark, showing exactly where the shell had landed. So the gunnery officer merely stepped up his shots to the flashes. Anyway, they stopped firing.

DRAMATIC ESCAPE

The night that HMS *Amethyst* made her dramatic run to freedom, George Oliver was on radio watch on *Belfast*. It was his job to monitor and pass on the situation reports ('sitreps') that followed the escaping ship's progress down the Yangtze.

In the early part, sitreps were received regularly: *Amethyst* slipping away under cover of two river boats; proceeding without incident; shore batteries opening up; one of the river boats hit and on fire; approaching the control boom; being challenged by the shore authorities; getting through the boom in the wake of another river boat; and so on.

Then came an uncomfortable period when no sitreps were received, but eventually we got the signal we were all waiting for – *Amethyst* had rejoined the Fleet . . . after many long, hot months as prisoners of the Chinese.

MAIN DECK

When she was carrying her full wartime complement, HMS *Belfast* was home to almost a thousand souls. Not a comfortable home by any means, but a place where men could eat, drink, sleep, work, relax and, most importantly of all, fight when the need arose.

New ratings would have arrived on board via the **Quarterdeck** — just as you do today, except that they would have saluted when doing so. For the rest of their time on ship, most of the men could only walk the boards of the Quarterdeck again if they had special reason — to attend a PT class, for example, or a Sunday church service presided over by the captain. Otherwise the Quarterdeck was usually reserved for officers, a long-standing tradition in Royal Navy ships, possibly because its position towards the stern made it the most sheltered of the ship's open spaces when under way.

DID YOU KNOW?

The ship's motto is 'Pro Tanto Quid Retribuamus', which means 'What shall we give in return for so much?'. The sailors had a different translation: 'We give as good as we get.'

Cat napping (left)
On HMS *Belfast*, even the ship's cat had a hammock. Unlike some of the men in wartime, it did not have to take it in turns to use it.
IWM BELF429

Ship's bell (far left)
The silver bell hanging beneath the gun turret on the Quarterdeck was presented to the ship by the people of Belfast in 1948. The less valuable original was rung every half hour to mark the passing of each watch — a welcome sound at the end of a cold spell of duty.
Lent by Belfast City Council

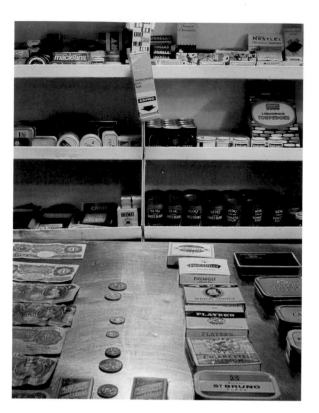

LIVING AND EATING

Following the ship's modernisation in the mid-1950s, almost every compartment on the same deck level as the Quarterdeck was assigned for the general use of the crew. This was where you would come to eat and drink, buy tobacco, pick up your mail and laundry, visit the **Sick Bay** or **dental surgery**, or pay a quiet visit to the **chapel**. It was also home to the **sound reproduction equipment room**, where, in the 1950s and 1960s, radio programmes were broadcast to entertain the crew.

The **galley** that you can see on HMS *Belfast* today was manned by trained staff. From the mid-1950s onwards you would queue up to be served food at the counter and then sit with your shipmates in the **Ship's Company Dining Hall** to eat it. To the men who served on board *Belfast* in the Second World War, this would have seemed like luxury. Back then, you would have been assigned with a few other men to a table or 'mess' somewhere on board the ship. One of your messmates would have been sent to the galley to prepare a basic meal and then they would have served it up at your mess, and cleared it up afterwards. You can see what a typical mess of this sort looked like in the **Arctic Messdeck**.

DID YOU KNOW?

The crew once ate rats for dinner. After a buffeting by Typhoon Ruth in 1962, soup was served in the dining hall. As the dregs were spooned out, four rat skulls appeared at the bottom of the pot. They had fallen into the soup from the ship's piping during the storm.

Kneading machine (left)
In the Far East, HMS *Belfast* was expected to act as 'mother' to any smaller ships sailing in her company. Each day, for example, a team of six bakers had to produce enough bread for several ships — not just for the hundreds of men on board *Belfast*.
IWM BELF418

NAAFI canteen (top left)
NAAFI stands for the Navy Army and Air Force Institute, which has provided canteen, entertainment and provision services to the armed forces since 1921. The NAAFI staff were the only civilians to serve in ships such as HMS *Belfast*.
IWM BELF433

HERO OF THE CANTEEN

Of all the men who served in HMS *Belfast* in the Second World War, it was arguably one of her civilian senior canteen assistants who contributed most to the Allied cause. Before he joined *Belfast*, Tommy Brown was a NAAFI worker on HMS *Petard*, when she helped to bring a U-boat to the surface and force its crew to abandon ship. The fifteen-year-old Brown and two others swam to the stricken U-boat and managed to retrieve documents that provided the key for breaking the German Enigma code. As a result the Allies were able to track U-boat movements and keep open the vital convoy route to Russia.

Brown was the only one of the three men to get out of the sub alive. For his bravery he was awarded the George Medal – one of the highest honours a civilian can gain in wartime. Sadly while on leave from *Belfast* in February 1945, Brown died trying to rescue his sister from a house fire in South Shields.

Tommy Brown, GM (left)
In the words of *Belfast* veteran Peter Rudd, Tommy Brown was 'a modest, unassuming chap'. His mother only learned about his medal when she was invited to London to receive it after his death.

Detail from the provision issue room (top)
For most men the provision issue room was the most important compartment in the entire ship. This was where the daily rum ration was measured and issued to each mess.
IWM BELF764

SLEEPING

Throughout most of HMS *Belfast's* lifetime, the sailors slept in hammocks slung just 52cm apart from each other in their messes. During the Second World War, when the number of crew rose from 761 to over 950, men had to look elsewhere for space to sleep.

Some slung their hammocks in inhospitable places like the **capstan machinery space**, home for the machinery that pulled up the ship's anchor. Others slept beneath mess tables, or had to share the use of a hammock with a man on a different watch. Radio Operator Arthur Ledbury can even recall sleeping across the top of some lockers after a particularly tiring spell on duty.

FIGHTING

Although the 'Main Deck' was predominantly about the living requirements of the men, it also served its purpose when the ship went into action. Looming over the Quarterdeck, for example, is **'Y' Turret** – one of the ship's four main turrets. Slightly further forward, and on the level above, is 'X' Turret, while 'A' and 'B' Turrets are located at the bow of the ship.

The Main Deck was also home to the ship's two torpedo mountings, one to port and the other to starboard. These were removed during the 1950s refit and the previously open ship's side was plated over, forming a new passageway. One curious result of this and other refits is that portholes that once opened out on to exterior walkways can now be found on the inner walls of more recently added corridors or compartments.

Capstan machinery space
(above)

Even in a place as inhospitable as the capstan machinery space, a night in a hammock was surprisingly comfortable. It would mould itself to your body and hold you still despite the motion of the ship.
IWM BELF440

DID YOU KNOW?

HMS *Belfast* is so long that you could almost lie Big Ben's clock tower along its decks . . . twice.

PUTTING THE ROYAL MARINES TO WORK

Like every large ship in the fleet, HMS *Belfast* carried a detachment of Royal Marines. They were the ship's soldiers, available to mount operations on land – as they did with distinction during the Korean War. But they had to pull their weight on board too. When the ship was at action stations, you would find a team of Marines manning the Transmitting Station, where all the gunnery control calculations were made, and another team manning 'X' Turret, where they enjoyed healthy competition with the seamen crews on 'A', 'B' and 'Y' Turrets. Tradition also dictated that everyday jobs such as butcher, postman and medical orderly were set aside for the Marines.

Entertaining the troops (left)
A separate contingent of Royal Marines provided *Belfast*'s band, seen here playing for troops ashore in Korea, September 1952.
IWM A32308

Mark IX torpedo (top)
An example of a 21-inch Mark IX torpedo is still on display in one of the Main Deck corridors.
IWM BELF763, IWM BELF761

In their own words

A great deal of the ship's life was played out on the level of the **Main Deck** — from the ceremony of the Quarterdeck to the daily concerns of laundry and sleeping. Here a few veterans recall the memories that these areas evoke . . .

CAUGHT IN AN EXPLOSION

Veteran George Woodley, **who was a boy seaman on board HMS** *Belfast* **in 1939, recalls what it felt like on the Main Deck when a magnetic mine exploded beneath the ship's hull as she undertook manoeuvres for a practice shoot in the Firth of Forth.**

I went for'rd to the fo'c'sle mess deck. I was standing at the bottom of a ladder when an explosion lifted me some feet in the air, jarring my teeth and chipping them. The lights went out and there was a deathly silence. I rushed up on deck to find many bewildered men milling around.

There was a man under punishment confined to cells. The Royal Marine sentry was thrown across the capstan engine by the explosion and was badly injured, but he managed to crawl to the cells and release the prisoner. After that, cells at sea were never locked during the war.

Boy Seaman David Bedford was in the telephone exchange when the explosion occurred and the exchange became flooded. Water was up to his waist but he remained at his post until he was evacuated.

MIXING WITH ROYALTY

The Quarterdeck was also the scene of many official visits to HMS *Belfast*, **including two by King George VI during the Second World War.** Lieutenant W P Brooke Smith **recalls both visits in his diary.**

The King was piped on board by six quartermasters and then walked round the Divisions. My division was the first to be inspected. I was introduced and shook hands and then took the King round.

He walks at a terrific rate and as the whole visit was timed to a schedule we had instructions to delay him for three minutes. I introduced the youngest Boy in the ship to him — Boy Wallis, aged sixteen — and made a heroic rear rank stand by pointing out another Boy who had only been in the ship a few days — but as soon as the King stopped to talk to him I realised that the Boy had been in the ship for months! A sticky moment but it passed off all right.

> **'I was introduced ... and then took the King round. He walks at a terrific pace!'**

Visit by the King (above)
Watched by the crew of HMS *Belfast*, King George VI shakes hands with the ship's captain before leaving the ship. In the foreground is the ship's detachment of Royal Marines on the Quarterdeck.
IWM A18665

And on the second visit . . .

One funny episode occurred on the Quarterdeck when the King remarked to the captain how clean the ship was. He then put his hands on the guardrail and leaned over to watch the drifter coming alongside [to take him to shore]. Then he looked at his hands and they were covered with black oil as the wires had just been painted. "I see I spoke too soon," was his comment.

TORPEDOES AWAY!

HMS *Belfast* no longer carries torpedo tubes but Lieutenant E Palmer recalls how he believed the type of torpedo displayed on the Main Deck may have played a part in the sinking of *Scharnhorst* in December 1943.

We had to fire from just outside 6,000 yards and that's rather long to be certain of hitting. However, we got one hit, and turned to fire the port tubes, but by the time the sights came on she'd sunk.

The tubes' crews had a better view of her than I. Being low down they saw *Scharnhorst* silhouetted against the clear sky and both saw and felt the explosion when the torpedo hit. We're painting a swastika on 'X' tube, from which the hitting torpedo came!

THIRST FOR TROUBLE

The Sick Bay on HMS *Belfast* saw a good deal of use during the Korean War – but, when water supplies were low, some 'patients' were just trying to quench their thirst, as Surgeon Lieutenant Rowan explains.

On one occasion, when the heat and the huge consumption of drinking water had driven the engineers to turn off the supply, a dishevelled and sweaty face appeared around the Sick Bay door and asked for two aspirin. With the usual Sick Bay courtesy he was given these but was refused a glass of water to swallow them with. He left the aspirin and departed, still thirsty.

During the Battle of Changni-do, when the bay was strewn with stretchers and blood lay thick, a brave sailor penetrated past the notices on the Sick Bay door and again requested two aspirin. It is said that he avoids the Sick Bay these days!

Winning team (right)
The torpedomen of light cruiser HMS *Jamaica* enjoy a break after their crucial role in the sinking of *Scharnhorst*. The torpedo crews on board HMS *Belfast* also played their part towards the end of the battle.
IWM A21167

Prisoners of war (right)
Three enemy soldiers are held under armed guard on the Quarterdeck in September 1951.
IWM HU36585

'The surgeon asked me if I was squeamish about blood.'

WAR IN THE SICK BAY

Crewmen on HMS *Belfast* tended to have more than one set of duties to perform. Veteran Ray Long was a Stoker Mechanic but also helped out in the Sick Bay. Here he remembers one particularly long and trying night during the Korean War.

I was in the Sick Bay on light duties when North Korean prisoners were brought on board, including some that were badly wounded. The Surgeon began operating late in the evening. As the light from the overhead lights was very dim, I was sent to get a damage-control battery light by our Surgeon. He told me to hold it up, directing it to the operating table. He asked me if I was squeamish about blood. Gritting my teeth, I replied, 'No, Sir'.

I witnessed the most horrible sights, with limbs being removed and serious head wounds operated on. A young girl soldier from South Korea, with bayonet wounds on both sides of her upper body, was lying in a cot next to a North Korean soldier who had his leg in plaster from a bullet wound. The girl got hold of a scalpel, on a tray next to her cot, and tried to stab him. He was removed from the Sick Bay and taken to a temporary prison in the diving locker room and guarded by the Royal Marines.

We spent all night in the Sick Bay, cleaning up after every operation and looking after the wounded. At about 04:30, we broke for refreshments and the Surgeon and the anaesthetist took us into the Surgeon's office, where we were given a beer each and very rare beef sandwiches. Somebody must have had a macabre sense of humour, as we had seen enough blood for one day!

DID YOU KNOW?
So many prisoners were taken on one day during the Korean War that many had to be held in the ship's meat store.

35

WHITER THAN WHITE?

The laundry that you can see on HMS *Belfast* today was only added in the 1950s. Before then 'dhobi-ing', as the men called it, was a bit more basic. Brian Butler who served as a boy seaman on the ship during the Second World War remembers it well.

Laundry? We never had a laundry. You had your bucket . . . and long yellow bars of soap and that was all you had to do your washing with. You could go down to the bathroom and have a shower and you took your bucket down with you and sat with nothing on, on a stool down there, and did your dhobi-ing in a bucket.

Some of it was a bit grey, I can tell you, especially where we had these blue serge jumpers where the dye used to come out and get into our white singlets. But they were clean you know — they smelt fresh!

Washing day (left)
Men of HMS *Wolverine* take advantage of some good weather to do a spot of 'dhobi-ing' – naval slang for clothes washing – on deck during a spell in harbour at Freetown, Sierra Leone, 1943.
IWM A22951

FIRST NIGHT ON BOARD

When HMS *Belfast* carried her full wartime complement of men, space was at a premium. The 2nd Baron Moran, son of Churchill's personal doctor, served in the ship as an ordinary seaman in 1943. In his memoirs he recalls the struggle to find a place of his own.

When a man joins a club, he quickly learns which chairs are reserved for older, more distinguished members. After joining *Belfast* I soon discovered that the same principle applied to the slinging of hammocks.

I had to wait until the other hammocks were slung and then wander forward through a maze of watertight doors and small compartments, searching for a vacant spot. I had to leave the warmth of the messdecks altogether and establish myself in the capstan flat, a large, cold space cluttered up with cable-winding machinery. Here I slept for the next month.

It was bitterly cold, and at night the banging of loose ice against the sides of the ship outside echoed through the flat, but I quickly found that a hammock is the warmest, as well as one of the most comfortable, of beds.

Time for bed (below)
A Second World War able seaman demonstrates the tricky art of swinging yourself into your hammock.
IWM A2216

Shell room

Replica 6-inch shells sit on a
revolving carousel ready to be
hoisted up to the gun turret.
The mechanism could deliver
up to ten shells per minute.

IWM BELF242

LOWER DECKS

Below the level of the Quarterdeck there are the three most heavily protected decks in the ship. The bottom two in particular benefit from the 10cm armoured plating on the sides of the ship and a 7.5cm reinforced deck immediately above. It is no surprise, then, to find that these decks house some of the ship's most vital organs – equipment that the ship could least afford to be hit.

The most important materials to keep away from enemy strikes were *Belfast's* stores of ammunition and explosives, which could blow the ship apart in an instant if they were hit. Each of the four 6-inch gun turrets was served by its own **shell room** and **magazine**, positioned in the bowels of the ship directly below each gun.

The cordite charges used to fire the shells were especially vulnerable, so they were stored in magazines buried in the **hold deck**, the lowest habitable level of the ship.

DID YOU KNOW?

Some crewmen knew they would be deliberately drowned if it meant saving the ship. If *Belfast* received a hit that threatened an explosion in the magazines, the area could be rapidly flooded to keep the vessel intact. The 22 men at action stations down there would have had little chance of escape.

39

Engine Room machinery
(right)
A pressure gauge from the Forward Engine Room
IWM BELF250

BELFAST UNDER POWER

BOILERS: FOUR ADMIRALTY 3-DRUM BOILERS, SMALL TUBE TYPE SUPERHEATERS AND PREHEATERS

ENGINES: FOUR PARSONS SINGLE REDUCTION GEARED TURBINES

SHAFT HORSEPOWER: 80,000

OIL FUEL CARRIED: 2,256 TONS (INCLUDING DIESEL OIL)

MAXIMUM SPEED (IN TRIALS): 32 KNOTS (36 MILES / 56 KM PER HOUR)

ECONOMICAL RANGE (USING 2 BOILERS AND 2 SHAFTS AT 10 KNOTS): 7,350 MILES

FULL POWER RANGE (USING 4 BOILERS AND 4 SHAFTS AT 30 KNOTS): 2,200 MILES

SOURCE OF POWER

In battle, a ship that cannot keep moving is dead in the water, so its propulsive machinery was also heavily protected. There were two boiler rooms on HMS *Belfast* paired with two engine rooms, all arranged in separate watertight compartments. If one boiler room was hit, the other could keep feeding its engine room — and a connection could be opened to feed the other engine room too. This meant that a single enemy hit could never disable more than 50 per cent of the ship's power plant, so allowing it to keep on the move.

The power generated by the boilers was also harnessed for other purposes. Most importantly it was used to drive the ship's turbo generators, providing the electric power needed to run the navigational, communications and gunnery systems that made *Belfast* such a formidable fighting force. It also drove the fire and bilge pump, which drew sea water into the ship's fire mains (ready to fight fire) and pumped out the noxious bilge that drained down to the bottom of the ship from other decks.

DID YOU KNOW?

The crewman steering *Belfast* couldn't see where he was going. Called the helmsman, he stood at the Forward Steering Position, deep in the lower decks of the ship, and took orders from an officer up on the Compass Platform.

Forward steering position (below)
The helmsman received instructions from an officer standing on the Compass Platform six decks above. Either side of the helmsman, two telegraph men transferred engine orders to the appropriate engine set.
IWM BELF431

ACTION STATIONS!

For most of their time at sea, the crew of HMS *Belfast* would have been at 'cruising stations', performing their day-to-day duties whenever they were on watch. But at any time of day or night, an alarm might sound throughout the ship calling the entire crew to 'action stations', meaning that contact with the enemy was either imminent or probable.

As soon as you heard the alarm, you would grab your lifejacket and any gear you needed for your particular action station (a helmet perhaps, or a pair of fire-retardant gloves), and report for your designated duty. Minutes after the alarm was sounded, everyone was expected to be in position and on alert, all the watertight doors between compartments would be shut, and the ship's guns would be ready to fire on command.

In for the long haul (left)

Members of a gun crew on HMS *Sheffield* are pictured at an intermediate state of readiness – staying in position at their action station but allowed to sleep, read or otherwise pass the time. This state of readiness would be ordered if the ship faced a prolonged period of danger such as on convoy duty in the Second World War.

IWM A6879

GUNNERY CONTROL

In the heat of battle, there was one small compartment on the lower decks that tended to operate in almost total silence. This was the **6-inch Transmitting Station**, built around a large mechanical computer called the **admiralty fire control table**.

Its function was to take in targeting information from the **Operations Room** and **Forward Director Control Tower** right at the very top of the ship and calculate the angles of train and elevation required by the gunners.

It took a small group of Royal Marines to operate the table, providing the brainpower to make the most of *Belfast*'s brawn.

6-inch Transmitting Station (right)

The job of manning the Admiralty Fire Control Table was one of the duties performed by HMS *Belfast*'s detachment of Royal Marines.

IWM BELF423

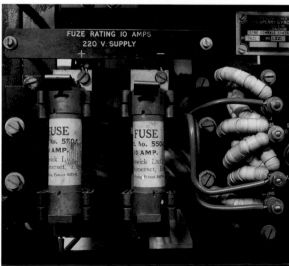

LOCKED IN COMBAT

When HMS *Belfast* went to action stations, a large proportion of the crew would scurry down ladders and through watertight doors to take up position in these lower deck compartments. For some this literally meant being locked in with no certainty of ever getting out again.

In the hours that followed, there might be no discernible activity and then bells would ring, lights would flash and orders would be barked across loudspeakers. There would be a frenzy of lever-pulling, button-pressing and valve-turning that might last for seconds, minutes or hours and then all would be quiet again. And in all that time, you might well have no idea what was happening.

Power conversion machinery (above)
HMS *Belfast* used both direct (DC) and alternating (AC) electric current to power her equipment. The AC current was used to supply items such as her gyro compass, gunnery control systems, radar and wireless equipment.
IWM BELF267

Inside a turbine (top)
One of the ship's high pressure turbines is displayed with its cover raised to show the rotary blades within.
IWM BELF752

The same was true during watches in lower states of readiness. Stoker Mechanic Dick Papworth remembers being in one of the engine rooms on a night-time watch during the Korean War. Hours passed by, the ship going steady, when suddenly the telegraph rang for an immediate STOP.

No sooner had Dick shut down the sprayers on the boilers, when the telegraph rang FULL and he was turning them back on. Then it was STOP again . . . and he finally had time to look for the shoe that he'd lost in all the commotion.

It was only later that he found out that an American troopship had been steaming straight for *Belfast* and she had had to take immediate evasive action. Such was life in the lower decks.

DID YOU KNOW?

Boiler rooms weren't always boiling hot. They were ventilated with air drawn from outside the ship, so in the Arctic they could be freezing cold.

Ship's Company Washrooms (above)
The washrooms between the forward boiler and engine rooms were added in the 1950s. Evaporators connected to the boiler system were used to distil sea water for washing and drinking.
IWM BELF421

LIFE ON WATCH

As a crewman on HMS *Belfast*, you would carry out your duties according to a regular watch schedule – four hours on, four hours off. The first watch would begin at 20:00 hours, followed by the middle watch at midnight, the morning watch at 04:00, the forenoon watch at 08:00 and the afternoon watch at 12:00. Between 16:00 and 20:00 was the dog watch, which was split into 2-hour sections. This allowed all the men to have their dinner, and ensured that every crew member had a different sequence of watches every other day. Once you got used to the system, it could be hard to adjust to civilian life – many veterans found themselves unable to sleep for more than four hours at a time for years afterwards.

Dressing for duty (left)
A look-out on HMS *Sheffield* pulls on layer after layer of clothing ahead of another watch in arctic conditions, December 1941.
IWM A6896

In their own words

Even today when you climb down ladder after ladder into the **Lower Decks** of HMS *Belfast*, it feels as though you are entering another world. In wartime, the feeling could be stranger still, as these veterans remember.

DANGER ABOVE AND BELOW

John Rowlett was an able seaman in October 1951 when Typhoon Ruth struck the coast of Japan, killing almost a thousand people. HMS *Belfast* had to ride the storm out at sea and John remembers risking broken limbs and worse to deal with a problem in the magazines.

'*We were in a full-scale hurricane and the ship was rolling and pitching all over the place.*'

We were in a full-scale hurricane and the ship was rolling and pitching all over the place. I was on watch and we were sent to secure anything on deck which might come adrift, or cause damage, or go over the side.

The weather got much worse and we had to heave to so that some 6-inch shells that had broken loose in the magazines could be made secure. The watch on deck, of which I was one, was sent down to put things right. You couldn't see the shells as somehow water had got into the magazine, but you could hear them as they crashed into the side as the ship rolled.

Some of the lads got up in the racks and when the shells had rolled up to one we jumped into the water, fished around until we found a shell, grabbed it, and handed it up to them in the racks. If you had time to grab another one you did and scrambled up in the shell racks before the shells rolled back again.

DID YOU KNOW?
If you entered a boiler room without using the airlock properly, the boiler could 'flash back' and incinerate everyone nearby.

Fire and ice (right)
Crewmen attend to the boilers on HMS *Inglefield* during escort duty in the Arctic. The outside temperature on deck was well below freezing point.
IWM A15408

TAKING A STEP INTO HELL

Conditions in the boiler rooms of HMS *Belfast* were tough. It was noisy, uncomfortable and generally hot. Here Ted Hill, a Junior Stoker during the Korean War, recalls what it was like to step through the airlock and into the atmosphere of the Boiler Room itself.

It's like taking a step into hell. There's four enormous fans sucking air from outside to maintain an air pressure and they make an horrendous noise when they're going full blast . . . And in the tropics, if it's 100 degrees outside, it's not cool air they're sucking in . . . I mean, you go down in a nice clean pair of overalls and when you come out in four hours' time they're absolutely sodden and sticking to you.

And if you wanted a pee, you did it in this tobacco tin and in the side of the boiler there was a little hatch. As soon as you opened it, the air rushed in and you could pour this tin of pee a few inches away from the hole and it would whip into the boiler. That's how we did it, you know!

STRESSFUL NIGHT AT THE WHEEL

Len Brice served on board *Belfast* in the late 1940s as a helmsman. Here he recalls what it was like to man the Forward Steering Position, trying to stay alert at the wheel of a cruiser weighing well over 14,000 tons.

It used to be a bit eerie, especially of a night-time, because there's less activity up on deck — just the Officer of the Watch or the Navigating Officer or his assistants would be there.

About every hour or so, they might change course. And the Officer of the Watch would say: 'Right, steer green two five zero.' To get that, he might give me manoeuvres by saying: 'Right, port fifteen' and you'd go to port fifteen and you'd hold for a while. And then the ship is gradually turning — don't forget the weight of the ship and the speed — it's not as if it's a little rowing boat!

When you're on that wheel, it's concentration the whole time. You can't afford to relax. You're just watching that compass. You know straightaway if you're off course for five minutes because the Officer of the Watch would be shouting down: 'Get on course, Brice!' Four hours on that, reading the compass, can be quite stressful ...

> '*I tried to count the number of ladders and the number of steps I went down.*'

LOST IN THE BOWELS OF THE SHIP

The first few hours on board a ship like HMS *Belfast* could be pretty daunting. Here Bob Shrimpton remembers being shown his action station on the ASDIC (submarine detecting equipment) and worrying that he might never find it again!

We went down all these flights of steps. I said: 'Where are we going?' He said: 'We're going to your action station.' 'What, down here?' He said: 'Yep, the ASDIC cabinet is down on the bilge plates.'

And I thought: 'Crikey!' And I tried to count the number of ladders and the number of steps I went down, and I thought: 'I'll have to get tremendously fit to get down all these, but at least I won't need a duffle coat down here!'

Men at work (left)
A rare photograph of a Royal Marine team in action at a Transmitting Station — much like the one on *Belfast*. It was taken on board the aircraft carrier HMS *Victorious* during the Second World War.
IWM A7640

EARNING A REPUTATION

When the Korean War broke out in 1950, it was the first time that HMS *Belfast* had fired her guns in anger since the Second World War. Here her Gunnery Officer Lieutenant Commander H G G Ogilvie remembers how one key component of the ship helped her become an instant hit — in more ways than one ...

The ship was fortunate in having a very good Fire Control Table manned by a most experienced Transmitting Station crew. We were usually able to put the first round of a shoot within 200 yards of a target and very soon were pouring in rapid broadsides in fire for effect. *Belfast* gained a name for rapid, accurate shooting, and hard hitting.

HERO BELOW THE WATERLINE

When HMS *Belfast* opened up her guns against *Scharnhorst* on 26 December 1943, she was only able to do so thanks to one man. Here Leading Stoker Larry Fursland explains how his actions earned him the Distinguished Service Medal.

Action stations sounded at 08:45 on St Stephen's Day. For the next 12 hours I was closed up in the port diesel compartment on my own.

I had never experienced a broadside before, and when the guns started firing, the vibrations and shuddering of the ship knocked the two circulating pumps out of action, allowing the generator to lose its cooling water and overheat. And loss of power would have affected the operation of the gun turrets.

'*I was just one person doing his duty as best as I could.*'

I wasn't able to communicate with the forward engine room by phone because of the noise level of the engines. However, I was aware of the fire main and hose that hung in the flat above, so I carried these down to the diesel compartment.

On the diesel bodywork was a screwed connection to take a hose coupling, but no tool to make the connection. I used my fingers and thumb to screw tight the coupling, hurting my hand in the process.

The diesel carried on running with its temporary water supply for the period that I was closed up. The only thing that worried me was being on my own. You could hear all the [reverberations] of the shell-fire and torpedoes and everything striking the side of the ship. And I was down the bottom . . .

I often think about that incident, but I realise that all my shipmates did their job well, and I was just one person doing his duty as best as I could.

A THOUGHT FOR THE ENEMY

Engineer Lieutenant Charles Simpson was in one of the engine rooms on HMS *Belfast*, when news came through that the Battle of North Cape was over. He remembers feeling sorry for the German crew.

When *Scharnhorst* was actually sunk, a smell came down the ventilation trunking of fuel oil, one of the foulest smells in all the world. I thought: 'Poor devils. Swimming in that, can you imagine?'

The lucky few
Blindfolded survivors of the *Scharnhorst* arrive at Scapa Flow on 2 January 1944, ready for transfer to prisoner of war camps. Only 36 of the battle cruiser's 1,963 men were pulled alive from the icy waters.
IWM A21201

UPPER DECKS

HMS *Belfast* was a floating gun platform and all the hundreds of men on board her were there for one purpose: to get the guns into position, aim them and fire them.

Most of the levels above the **Upper Deck** — collectively known as the ship's superstructure — were devoted to the careful coordination of these efforts. It is on these upper levels, therefore, that you find the brains of the ship — her navigational, tactical, communication and gunnery control systems — and the majority of the guns themselves.

In fact, HMS *Belfast* had more 'brains' than most ships because she was designed to be a flagship, carrying an admiral in charge of his fleet as well as a captain in charge of the ship. The ship therefore had a separate **Admiral's Bridge**. That way the admiral could exercise control over the fleet or squadron of vessels under his command without overcrowding the **Compass Platform** and **Operations Room**, where the captain was at work.

DID YOU KNOW?

If you stand on the deck of HMS *Belfast* for long enough, you could find yourself about six metres higher or lower than when you started, thanks to the tide on the River Thames.

51

Capstan and chain (left)
The capstans on the fo'c'sle are part of the machinery used to winch up the ship's anchors. If power was lost, some 144 men would be needed to operate the machinery manually, pushing against large wooden bars inserted into the capstans.
IWM BELF294

BELFAST UNDER POWER

STANDARD DISPLACEMENT: 11,553 TONS	
MAXIMUM DISPLACEMENT (WITH FULL FUEL LOAD): 14,325 TONS	
OVERALL LENGTH: 613 FEET 6 INCHES (187M)	
BEAM: 69 FEET (21M)	
DRAUGHT: 19 FEET 9 INCHES (6.1M)	
MAXIMUM MAST HEIGHT (FOREMAST, 1939): 144 FEET 9 INCHES (44M)	

THE SHIP'S ARMAMENT

Wherever you stand on the **Upper Deck** – in the stern, the bow or amidships – you are never far away from one of the ship's guns. HMS *Belfast*'s main armament was made up of her four 6-inch gun turrets, two in the stern and two in the bow. The bow turrets were designated 'A' and 'B', and the stern turrets were 'X' and 'Y'. It is in 'Y' Turret that you can enjoy the thrilling **'Gun Turret Experience: A Sailor's Story, 1943'**, which plunges you into the thick of the action during the Battle of North Cape in 1943.

Each of the four gun turrets housed three guns, which could be used against enemy targets at sea or on land and had a maximum range of about 14 miles. When veterans talk about firing a broadside, they mean firing all three guns in all four gun turrets at the same time. Given that each gun could fire up to eight rounds per minute, HMS *Belfast* was capable of unleashing salvo after deafening salvo of shells, sending shockwaves through the ship.

Between the funnels of HMS *Belfast*, you can see the four pairs of **4-inch guns** that make up her secondary armament. Until 1945 she had a third pair of these guns towards the stern on each side, but these were removed to make way for additional deckhouses. These 4-inch guns could be used to protect the ship from attack by enemy aircraft, and against surface targets. That's why they are referred to as High Angle/Low Angle guns. Each of the eight gun barrels could fire a maximum of 15-20 rounds per minute at targets up to 12 miles away.

'Firing' the 4-inch guns (above)
Living History volunteers simulate firing the 4-inch guns. The 30kg shells for the guns were taken from lockers nearby, which were kept stocked up from the ship's magazines below.
IWM BELF56

SPORTS ON BOARD SHIP

Gather together several hundred young men on board a ship and it's no surprise to find that they turn to sport when they need to blow off a bit of steam. Whenever HMS *Belfast* came into port for any length of time, her crew would challenge the locals to games of various types including football, athletics, basketball, cross country, boxing, softball, rugby, water polo, swimming, judo, sailing, shooting, cricket and hockey. On board ship, apart from regular physical training sessions, the men played a game peculiar to the Royal Navy called deck hockey. It was very much like a game of traditional hockey but with a coil of old rope as a puck, and a 'pitch' cluttered with all the obstacles presented by the ship's deck. And the way the veterans tell it, the rules of fair play weren't always vigorously applied . . .

Jolly hockey ships (left)
Officers of HMS *Kent* enjoy a free-for-all game of deck hockey during the Second World War. The players tried to have several 'pucks' to hand because so many ended up overboard.
IWM A7605

COMMAND AND CONTROL

It was from the **Compass Platform** that the captain or the officer of the watch controlled the ship at sea, passing steering or engine orders to the helmsman in the **Forward Steering Position** six decks below. The ship's course was plotted by the navigating officer and his assistants in the **Chart House** at the back of the Compass Platform, although the compass reading actually came from the **Forward Gyro Compass Room** buried deep within the ship.

The **Operations Room** was set up to provide the captain with the tactical information he needed to make well-informed decisions. Men at plotting areas around the room would monitor radar, sonar and intelligence reports to build up a picture of allied and enemy surface, submarine and air forces. And they would display that ever-changing picture on glass 'stateboards' ready for the captain to view.

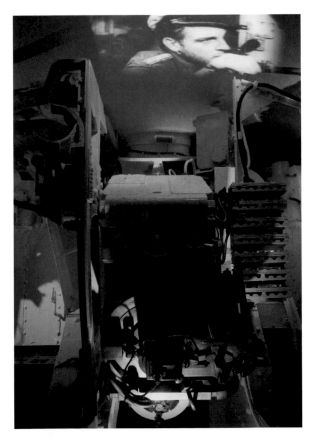

Gun Turret Experience (right)
Inside 'Y' Turret a combination of lights, sound, smoke effects and video projection takes you back in time to 1943 when 27 crewmen worked together in these cramped conditions to fire the ship's guns during the Battle of North Cape.
IWM BELF662

DID YOU KNOW?

If it was your job to keep the glass 'stateboards' up-to-date in the Operations Room, you had to be able to write backwards so that the officers on the other side could read it.

Think you could do it?

Ship's flags (right)
Two columns of flags fly above the ship. The one to the left of the photograph gives *Belfast*'s pendant number (C35), the one to the right her radio call sign (Golf, Golf, Charlie, November).
IWM BELF318

IDENTIFYING TARGETS

At the heart of what is now the **Operations Room** stood the gun direction area where, from 1942 onwards, officers and ratings would use radar to track and select the targets to be engaged by the ship's armament. Before HMS *Belfast* was fitted with radar, the only way to spot targets was by eyesight and this was done from the highest vantage point on the ship, the **Flag Deck**, home of the **Gun Direction Platform** and **Forward Director Control Tower**.

Perched in these exposed positions, lookouts would man four 'sights' and the captain a fifth on the centre platform — a sight was a set of binoculars mounted in a fixed but rotating position. The direction in which the sights were pointing was automatically relayed to the **Director Control Tower**, where a large optical range finder could be used to get a better fix on a possible target.

Fo'c'sle and anchor (left)
On HMS *Belfast* the forecastle or fo'c'sle was used primarily for the operation of the ship's anchors. *Belfast* originally carried three anchors, two on the starboard bow and one on the port. Only the port anchor is now stowed on the deck.
IWM BELF412

PLANE SAILING

To extend the ship's ability to locate targets, HMS *Belfast* was also designed to carry two reconnaissance seaplanes. These **Supermarine Walruses** were housed in hangars on the **Boat Deck** and launched by catapult to search for vessels beyond the horizon. After completing a flight, the aircraft would land in the sea alongside the ship and be lifted back on board by one of two cranes.

After the arrival of radar, there was no need to carry aircraft on board and the hangars were converted into additional accommodation.

Ship's crane (right)
The ship's crane was used for lifting boats on and off the Boat Deck, loading supplies, and – in wartime – for hoisting on board stretchers bearing wounded soldiers.
IWM BELF772

RUNNING A CRUISER

Running HMS *Belfast* was ultimately down to the ship's captain. It was his job to bring the ship into battle in good shape and make all the key tactical decisions. But the day-to-day operation of the ship was delegated to the ship's commander, known to the men as 'The Bloke'. Below him the chain of command took in scores of commissioned officers and hundreds of ratings all the way down to the lowliest boy seamen. Every officer and rating was assigned to a department of the ship; some, such as the Engine Room, accounting for 130 men; others, like the Medical Department, involving just a handful. Whatever your role, you had to know it inside out. Your captain and your fellow crewmen were relying on you.

Leaders of men (left)
A group of *Belfast* officers pose for a photograph in the 1940s. Officers made up less than a tenth of the ship's complement.
IWM A21370

In their own words

It's one thing to gaze at the city of London from the **Upper Decks** of HMS *Belfast* today, but as these stories show, it's quite another to watch enemy fire heading your way, or huge waves crashing over the bows of the ship . . .

CAROLS IN THE DARKNESS

As *Belfast* set out on 26 December 1943 to confront *Scharnhorst*, Lieutenant W P Brooke Smith was on duty at the top of the Director Control Tower. Here he recalls the strange atmosphere on board the ship.

The flagship had assumed a high degree of readiness which involved all personnel having action meals of bully-beef and biscuits at their action stations and snatching what sleep they could on the decks.

As usual, in those waters, the weather was bitterly cold and the sea was rough. These conditions could not dampen the spirits of my crew, perched in a director tower, exposed to the full force of the wind and the spray which was sweeping over the ship.

Towards evening, they became sentimental and struck up carols and soon other positions joined in, echoing 'Hark the Herald Angels Sing', 'The First Noel' and other old favourites out into the Arctic Sea.

CLOSE ESCAPE

The exposed deck areas of HMS *Belfast* were especially treacherous in rough seas, when huge waves would come sweeping over the ship. The conditions almost proved to be the end for Petty Officer John Harrison, but they also helped to save his life.

Our duty station was the Denmark Straits, backwards and forwards to stop German ships getting out. Now, the Denmark Straits is pretty cold and the cold is the only reason I'm here.

One early morning I wanted to get to 'A' Turret on the upper deck. Waiting for the big ones to come over and there's always a slack one after that and I dashed, got my hand on the gun turret door, opened the thing and a big one came over, swept me off my feet. But I didn't get washed overboard because my hand was frozen on the turret handle. And whenever I look at that handle now, I get a feeling . . .

Cold calling (right)
Signal projectors were used on the Flag Deck to send Morse code messages to other vessels. In this picture taken in 1941, a build-up of ice on the projector is making life hard for the signalman.
IWM A6872

IN THE FIRING LINE

Signalman Lance Tyler **was on duty on the Flag Deck of HMS** *Belfast* **during the Battle of North Cape.**

'A piece of shrapnel the size of a half-horseshoe dropped between us onto the flag deck.'

I was standing with a boy signalman some three feet apart, keeping an eye on *Sheffield* and *Norfolk*, on our port quarter, for signals; *Scharnhorst* was in the distance, off our starboard bow.

Suddenly, *Scharnhorst* fired a broadside, which missed our port side by a matter of feet. A piece of shrapnel the size of a half-horseshoe dropped between us onto the Flag Deck. Fortunately neither of us was hurt. However, we both learned that you do not pick up hot shrapnel, even in mid-winter in the Arctic. We both nursed burnt fingers for some weeks.

A HARSH LESSON

Manning a 4-inch gun could be a risky business, especially if it was your job to ram the shell into the breech by hand. The trick was to keep your fist clenched and to pull it out quickly. Unfortunately seventeen-year-old Boy Seaman John Campbell had to learn this the hard way as this 'Certificate for Wounds and Hurts' explains.

These are to certify the Right Honourable the Lords Commissioners of the Admiralty that Campbell, John (Boy, P/JX:154740) belonging to His Majesty's Ship *Belfast* being actually upon His Majesty's Service in carrying out gun drill at a 4-inch H.A. gun was injured on 18 August 1939 by allowing his right middle finger to become caught between the moving breech-block and the base of the practice cylinder thereby sustaining accidental traumatic amputation of the first two phalanges.

Into the breech (below)
A twin 4-inch gun crew practising during the Second World War. It was while operating one of these guns that Boy Seaman John Campbell suffered his injury.
IWM A16317

> ## *'sustaining . . . traumatic amputation of the first two phalanges.'*

D-DAY DUST-UP

Rear-Admiral Sir Morgan Morgan-Giles captained HMS *Belfast* in the early 1960s and led the campaign to preserve her as a museum ship. Here he relays a story told about an incident on the bridge during D-Day.

HMS *Belfast* was the flagship of Cruiser Squadron. She was running in on a very careful bearing when suddenly a rusty little mine-sweeper crossed right ahead of her from port to starboard.

To avoid cutting this little ship in half, HMS *Belfast* had to alter course violently to port — and of course this upset the gunnery calculations.

The Admiral was purple with rage and sent a furious signal to the young Sub Lieutenant in command of the mine-sweeper: **HAVE YOU A COPY OF THE RULES OF THE ROAD ON BOARD?**

After a few moments came the reply: **YES. WHAT IS IT YOU WISH TO KNOW!**

BEATING THE COLD

HMS *Belfast* originally carried two cranes on the Boat Deck for recovering the ship's Walrus aircraft after they had landed in the sea, but they also had other important tasks as Able Seaman R W Brown remembers.

DID YOU KNOW?

The baths on HMS *Belfast* had four taps — two for fresh water and, if that was scarce, two for salt.

In December 1943, on our way to Murmansk, we anchored in Seydisfjord, Iceland, and I spent a forenoon watch on the crane. It was very cold with a strong wind and a six-foot swell.

A boat came alongside, with an injured man in a basket stretcher who needed medical treatment. The crane had a heavy hook and, with the boat bouncing about, I was concerned that the hook might drop onto the stretcher, but the boat's crew managed to get the stretcher's sling onto the hook and I got the casualty on board safely.

'That was my first taste of rum and it lit a fire in my belly.'

I was chilled to the bone, and when relieved, I was late getting below for lunch. A three-badge able seaman asked me where I had been, and when I told him, he handed me his rum issue and said: 'Here, you need this more than I do.'

That was my first taste of rum and it lit a fire in my belly, which warmed me up. I don't recall the able seaman's name, but I've never forgotten his kindness.

RIDING OUT A STORM

Standing on the bridge today, it's hard to imagine that you might have to look up to see the sea, rather than down. But that's what John Wills, a member of the Admiral's staff remembers, when he was serving on board *Belfast* in the mid-1950s.

We had an occasion to thank this old girl. We went through a typhoon called Ruth — the worst rough weather I've ever seen. In fact, I went up on to the bridge . . . and I'm looking *up* at the water. It's not down there, it's up there!

I watched the nose going into what we call a big green one and you think she's not going to come up — she can't come up from this one! And up she comes and it gives you great confidence in your ship. We lost no men. What we did lose was masses of paint. She was stripped of all paint down the side.

DID YOU KNOW?

One Arctic storm was so strong, it ripped the roof off one of HMS *Sheffield*'s gun turrets. HMS *Belfast* came through it unscathed.

Looking up at the sea (right)
The view from the open bridge of HMS *Sheffield* as she fought her way through heavy seas on convoy duty in February 1943.
IWM A14890

'I watched the nose going into a big green one and you think she's not going to come up — she can't come up from this one!'

HMS BELFAST & YOU

If you have enjoyed your visit to HMS *Belfast*, there are several ways to extend that experience – both on the day and on future occasions – and to share it with family, friends or colleagues.

LEARNING ON HMS *BELFAST*

Exploring HMS *Belfast* is a unique learning environment in which to discover what life was like on board a warship during the Second World War and the Cold War. Schools can book a self-directed visit which can support subject areas such as humanities and art and design. Activities for families, schools and youth groups are available at certain times of the year.

For further information please visit: **iwm.org.uk/visits/hms-belfast/groups-schools**

KIP IN A SHIP

Kip in a Ship offers an exciting and affordable sleepover experience for schools and youth groups with children aged 7–18 in the heart of London. Participants can immerse themselves in the ship's history by sleeping overnight in real sailors' bunks.

For further information please visit: **iwm.org.uk/sleepover**

CORPORATE & PRIVATE HOSPITALITY

HMS *Belfast* is a city-centre venue with a difference. Moored in her prime location between London Bridge and Tower Bridge, the ship offers spectacular 360 degree views of the capital.

Guests can dine in the Officers' Mess, climb a gun turret or watch the sun set on the Quarterdeck. There are several spaces available, for boardroom meetings for up to 20 guests, conferences or banquets for up to 150, and spectacular parties for up to 450 guests during the summer on the outside decks.

To find out more, call **020 7403 6246** or email **hmsbelfast@iwmevents.co.uk**

VOLUNTEERING

Are you interested in helping to keep HMS *Belfast* in ship-shape condition? If so, we have opportunities for volunteers in a number of departments.

You could join our conservation team, fighting off the ever-present danger of corrosion, and helping to restore specific sections or equipment on the ship. Or become one of our Interaction Volunteers, offering visitors a friendly introduction to key spaces on the tour, such as the Compass Platform, and giving them the chance to handle authentic and replica equipment and uniforms.

You could also work behind-the-scenes to help with office support, or join volunteers from the Royal Naval Amateur Radio Society, operating radio equipment in the ship's Bridge Wireless Office.

If you would like to find out more please go to **iwm.org.uk/connect/volunteers/london-branches**

REFRESHMENTS

Take a break on board HMS *Belfast* in **The Café** with our range of sandwiches, kids' lunch bags, hot and cold drinks and freshly baked cakes and muffins. Have an ice cream on the boat deck and enjoy the river views in the summer months.

Alternatively, **Tom's Kitchen Deli**, from chef Tom Aikens, offers options for breakfast and lunch including freshly prepared sandwiches, soups, salads and homemade cakes. The Deli is located in the quayside pavilion, providing a stunning riverside location.

Above the Deli, **Tom's Kitchen Bar**, open daily from midday till late, offers spectacular views of HMS *Belfast* and Tower Bridge. The bar is part covered and part open air, so you can enjoy al fresco drinking overlooking the Thames. The all-day bar menu offers a delicious line-up of cocktails, spirits, beers and wines to enjoy, as well as seasonal sharing boards. For more information or to book a table please visit **iwm.org.uk**

SHOPPING

HMS *Belfast's* shop provides a wide range of contemporary and inspiring gifts, books, clothing and accessories, posters, stationery and souvenirs. For our younger visitors we have an exciting range of games, toys and children's books. For group school bookings, gift bags can be reserved in advance (online with group booking only) and paid for at the end of the visit. You can also browse our ranges online at **iwmshop.org.uk**

All retail proceeds help support IWM and its work.

ABOUT IWM

IWM is a global authority on conflict and its impact, from the First World War to the present day, in Britain, its former Empire and Commonwealth. We were created to record and showcase people's experiences of modern conflict. Some of those experiences paint a picture of everyday life in wartime; others give us a glimpse of something exceptional. All of them help us to explore the causes of war and its impact on people's lives. Using our unique collections, we engage audiences of all ages from across the world through our website **iwm.org.uk**, and at our five branches. As a charity, we rely on admissions fees, sales in our shops (including **iwmshop.org.uk**), cafés and donations to carry out our work and ensure that the stories of those who have lived, fought and died in conflicts since 1914 continue to be heard.

IWM LONDON

In Summer 2014 **IWM London** re-opened with a transformed new atrium, designed by architects Foster + Partners, as well as ground-breaking new First World War Galleries to mark the 100 year anniversary of the start of the Great War. The 'new' IWM London reveals more of IWM's unique collections, telling important stories of people's experiences of war and conflict up to the present day, including how conflict has divided communities in places such as Ireland, Iraq and Afghanistan.
Lambeth Road, London SE1 6HZ. Information **020 7416 5000**

IWM NORTH

The multi-award-winning **IWM North** was designed by world-renowned architect Daniel Libeskind to represent a globe shattered by conflict. The iconic building houses innovative and dynamic exhibitions, including hourly digital media *Big Picture Shows,* designed to explore how war shapes lives. It also plays host to a changing, free temporary exhibition programme and regular public events, with the aim of inspiring knowledge and encouraging debate.
The Quays, Trafford Wharf Road, Manchester M17 1TZ. Information **0161 836 4000**

IWM DUXFORD

Set within the best-preserved Second World War airfield in Europe, **IWM Duxford** is a vibrant museum that marries its fascinating past with contemporary displays, interactive exhibitions, working hangars and airfield and exciting events. Come and wander amongst two hundred aircraft to discover the fascinating human stories behind the machines that changed our lives forever. With one of the finest collections of tanks, military vehicles and artillery in the UK, we also show the impact of technological development on war and conflict.
Cambridgeshire, CB22 4QR. Information **01223 835 000**

CHURCHILL WAR ROOMS

Inside **Churchill War Rooms** lie the original Cabinet War Rooms – the secret underground bunker which sheltered Churchill and his staff during the Second World War. Explore the historic rooms, including the Map Room where the books and charts are exactly where they were left when the door was locked in 1945. Discover the stories of those who worked underground as London was bombed above them, and explore the life and legacy of Winston Churchill in the Churchill Museum.
Clive Steps, King Charles Street, London SW1A 2AQ. Information **020 7930 6961**

iwm.org.uk